AF443728

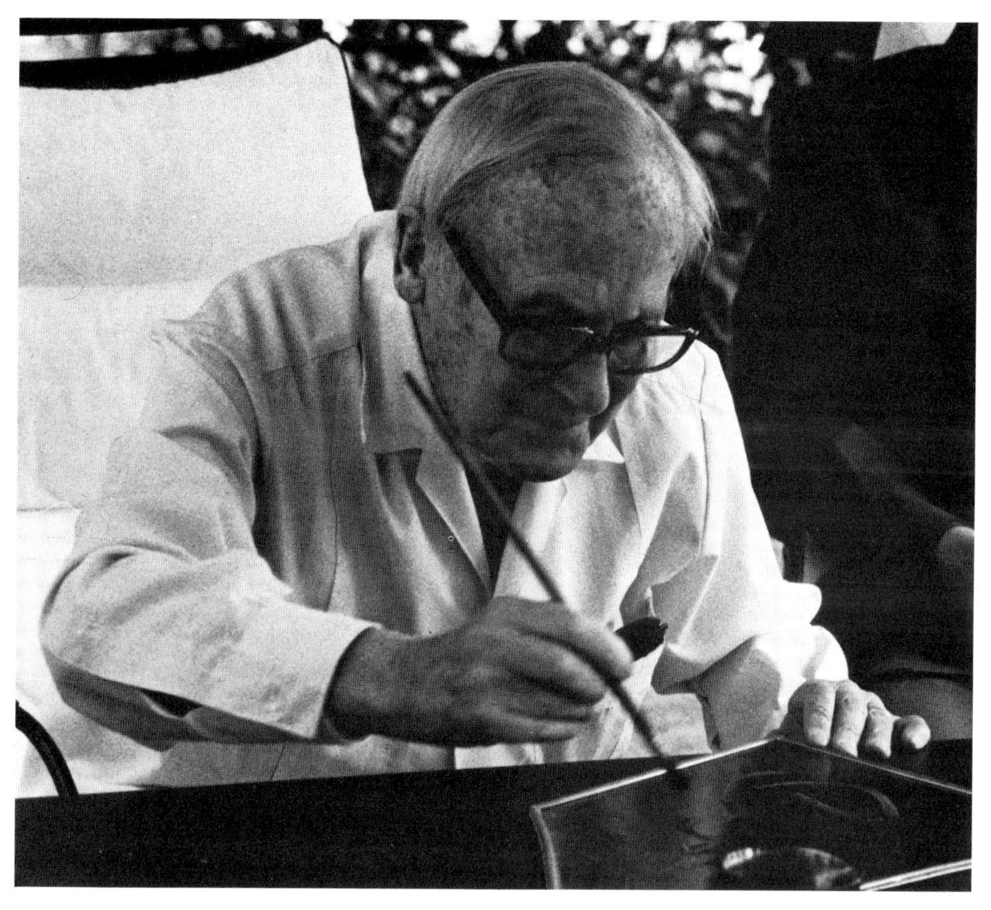

Waddington Galleries

2 and 4 Cork Street London W1X 1PA Telephone: 01-439 1866
Daily 10am-5.30pm Saturdays 10am-1pm

1 December-23 December 1981

Until the present exhibition, a substantial group of bronze sculptures by Miró had been seen in London only once, at the Hayward Gallery early in 1972. The large retrospective held at the Tate in 1964 happened just too early to include works from that burst of intense sculptural activity which began in 1966 and which, at the last count, has led to the making of about two hundred and fifty bronzes, some of them on a monumental scale. The Tate exhibition did, however, show a selection of Miró's ceramics, and with his work in this medium it has become customary to open any account of Miró's remarkably impressive achievement as a sculptor.

Miró's earliest ceramic pieces date from 1944 when the artist was living in Barcelona. They were produced under the guidance of his old friend the potter Joseph Llorens Artigas. A second, more imaginative period of collaboration followed in the early 1950's when Miró's shapes broke free from a dependence on function and became objects in their own right – heads, funny little *personnages*, ideas for monuments, their rough surfaces often incised and brightly coloured. During the initial phase of working with Artigas Miró started to model in clay small heads and other effigies, some of which were cast in bronze in 1950. The first to be cast were the two birds *Oiseau (Lunaire)* and *Oiseau (Solaire)* of 1944-6, each less than nine inches in height. Twenty years later they were transposed to a much larger scale – *L'Oiseau Lunaire* (1966) is nearly eight feet high – and as such they have become the grandest, best known and probably best loved of all Miró's sculptures.

In 1949 Miró also modelled a series of women, one of which is shown here (cat. 1). It is an important work, possessing qualities which owe as much to Miró's background in Surrealism as to his more recent experiments with the ceramic form. Its modest size, container-like shape and deeply scored surface suggest the latter, while the sculpture as a whole resembles one of those primitive fetishes or fertility symbols which the Surrealists were in the habit of spotting. The flowing lines and swelling forms recall Arp (this is especially obvious in the two bird sculptures) although Miró's allusion to the sexuality of

his creature is more explicit and wittier than anything we might find in Arp. *Femme* (1949) looks forward to the two women of 1967 (cats. 2 and 4) where the female sexual organ assumes a more definite shape and an even greater prominence; here the few neat cuts beneath the dark orifice are a plastic equivalent for the graphic language developed by Miró in his painting. As with the prototype of 1949, there is an ambiguity about the status of these two sculptures. Cat. 4 is just over a foot high – in other words, table-top size – and its basic form is that of a bell; turned on its head it would look like one of those lamps which Giacometti designed for Jean-Michel Frank in the early 1930s. The curve of the green patinated cat. 2 is more skirt-shaped but it also evokes a cup or vessel of some sort, placed lip downwards. Both are symmetrical and yet conceived fully in the round. The urge to pick up, almost to use, these objects is strong; the knob- and handle-like protuberances seem to invite such an activity, whereas really these breasts, bumps, indentations and marks give the feeling that Miró's curious inventions pulsate with a life of their own.

Biomorphic imagery, with its exaggeration of anatomical features reminiscent of Picasso, is characteristic of other works besides the bird and woman sculptures: *Conque* (cat. 12), the Ubuesque *Femme chien* (cat. 21) and the small bull's head of 1975 (cat. 26), the most recent piece in the exhibition. The original source for all such free, hybrid forms was probably Picasso's eight inch high figure *Metamorphosis* of 1928 (Musée Picasso 261 and 262), which dates from a time when the work of the two artists was running in closely parallel directions. But the bulk of Miró's three-dimensional output since 1950, when his first modelled sculptures were cast, has been of a very different kind, at least in terms of materials and technique. It relates not so much to the organic forms and rhythms of his painting but to the handful of Surrealist constructions and 'poetic objects' which he made around 1930, some of which had markedly sadistic overtones. A violent or aggressive pictorial language was not unique to Miró at this date: it can be found in works by Giacometti, Masson and Picasso, to name the most obvious. In Picasso's small relief of the summer of 1930, *Composition with Glove* (Musée Picasso 123), an analogy is drawn between the female genitals and the teeth of a trap. This is one of a series of assemblages which Picasso made by sticking found objects and scraps of material onto the backs of tiny stretched canvases and covering them with sand. Another work from this series, *Bather and Profile* (Musée Picasso 125), seems to have given Miró the idea for his slightly larger bronze relief of 1968, *Tête* (cat. 8), with its cheeky snout and childlike shorthand for hair and eyes.

As with Miró, there is a distinction to be made in Picasso's *oeuvre* between those sculptures which sing of a certain amplitude, of sweeping curves and dissolving forms, and those which make use of jagged scrap metal, old toys, utensils and similar bits of junk. Picasso's intervention in his bronzes of the late 1940s and early 1950s, however, is often extensive. Miró, on the other hand, is usually content to let the found objects speak for themselves. Strange disjunctions and dislocations in his sculptures imply that their author is closer to the spirit of Dada – for instance, the late work of Schwitters – than Picasso ever was in his attitude to mean or ephemeral materials.

In an interview with Dean Swanson published ten years ago, Miró was asked if he 'collected' objects. He replied: 'No, I just use things I find; I gather things together in my studio, which is very large. I place the objects around the floor, and choose this or that. I combine several objects, and sometimes re-use elements of other sculptures'.[1] Thus, the *croissant* which describes the sunflower head of *Femme Soleil* (cat. 6) reappears in *Sa Majesté* (cat. 5) where it suggests a crown or perhaps a ruff. In both sculptures the shape has erotic connotations – the equation of facial with sexual features was a classic Surrealist device. In other works we can recognise a toy speed boat (cat. 14), a waste outlet, a pair of doll's legs and some old nails left over from the casting process (cat. 16), tin cans, metal tubes, bottle tops and corks (cat. 19), the end of a rake or agricultural implement (cat. 9), and a nut and bolt, an electric bell and various lengths of bent wire (cat. 15).

In most cases these elements are metaphors for parts of the body. In the small version of *L'Equilibriste* (cat. 16), for example, the perforated drain becomes the juggler's stomach, while his left foot (he is standing on his head) balances a typical Miró creation, birdlike and probably female, complete with crescent moon. Other recurring forms in Miró's sculpture include horns and antennae (positive) and slits and wider openings (negative). There are no preliminary drawings: Miró works directly from the objects, feeling them, joining them, which is not unlike Henry Moore's practice since the late 1950s of working from hand-size maquettes, many of which have had as their starting-point a found stone or bone fragment. Miró has recalled how his sense of touch was awakened whilst a young student at art school in Barcelona: 'Francisco Galí was a remarkable teacher, and he gave me an exercise so that I would learn to "see" form: he blindfolded me, and placed objects in my hands, then asked me to draw the objects without having seen them.'[2]

Not all Miró's *objets trouvés* remain recognisable: their identities can be changed or simply suppressed. John Ashbery caught that feeling of mild disorientation mixed with a certain *frisson* with which we confront some of Miró's raw materials, when he wrote: 'They could be old machine parts dredged up from the limbo of a rural Catalan garage, or objects become anonymous through rust and weathering, or nameless parts of the ground: sticks, pebbles, clumps of leaf mould. And thus one has an agreeable sensation of being lost in a crowd of people who are somehow strange and familiar at the same time'.[3]

A number of Miró's sculptures are cast directly from objects using the lost wax process, the artist drawing on the wax impression before the bronze cast is made. It may seem paradoxical that Miró should wish to see his works, put together by chance out of humble materials with all the freshness and humour of a child's perception, preserved forever in the most durable of all metals; and yet their spontaneous, playful appeal is seldom lost in this transformation. Several of the bronzes are painted in shining colours – red, green, yellow, blue. Others rely on patina for their effect. Miró supervises closely the casting of his sculptures and is keenly aware of the different patinas available at different foundries. Those cast by Susse outside Paris (e.g. the modelled sculptures cats. 2, 4, 12 and 26) are the smoother, more polished, more traditional looking, whereas the pieces cast by Parellada in Barcelona (those incorporating junk objects) have a crude lack of finish which Miró finds attractive. *Femme Soleil* (cat. 6), for instance, is streaked a mottled yellowy grey and resembles some ancient goddess in stone. Both it and *Femme dans la Nuit* (cat. 3) actually stand on what appear to be rough stone bases – hollowed out in the case of the latter work. Other sculptures with this almost primeval look are the small *L'Equilibriste* (cat. 16) and *Projet pour un Monument* of 1969 (cat. 14).

Schemes for monuments are numerous in Miró's sculptural thinking and even those which do not include the word in their title very often imply an environmental dimension. *Femme dans la Nuit* (cat. 3) and *Femme Echevelée* (cat. 15) are both, in their different ways, flat, geometric images (cat. 3 has a cubist feel to it) which are best viewed squarely from the front or back. It is not difficult to imagine either of them sited on top of a distant hill, where they would assume the presence of primitive totems. The same goes for several other figures and *personnages* by Miró. The recurrence of birds, dogs, the moon, the sun and other symbols, frequently coupled with women, reminds us that Miró has never deserted the world of Surrealist archetypes. It is a nocturnal region – the setting for Ernst's *Revolution by Night* (1923) – where unspeakable things may happen: we have only to think of Giacometti's *Anguished Woman in her Room at Night* (1931-2). Miró's *Homme et Femme dans la Nuit* (cat. 13) must at one level be read as an overt tribute to the greatest of all Surrealist sculptors who belonged only briefly to the movement. And yet Miró's vision of the world is also unique, shaped by a combination of infantile fantasy, quickness and the ability to perceive things afresh, to start every time from scratch. There is much we can instinctively respond to in these sculptures.

1. 'The Artist's Comments, Extracts from an interview with Joan Miró', in catalogue of *Miró Sculptures*, Walker Art Center, Minneapolis, 1971.

2. Ibid.
3. 'Miró's Bronze Age', *Art News*, May 1970, p.36

© Richard Calvocoressi

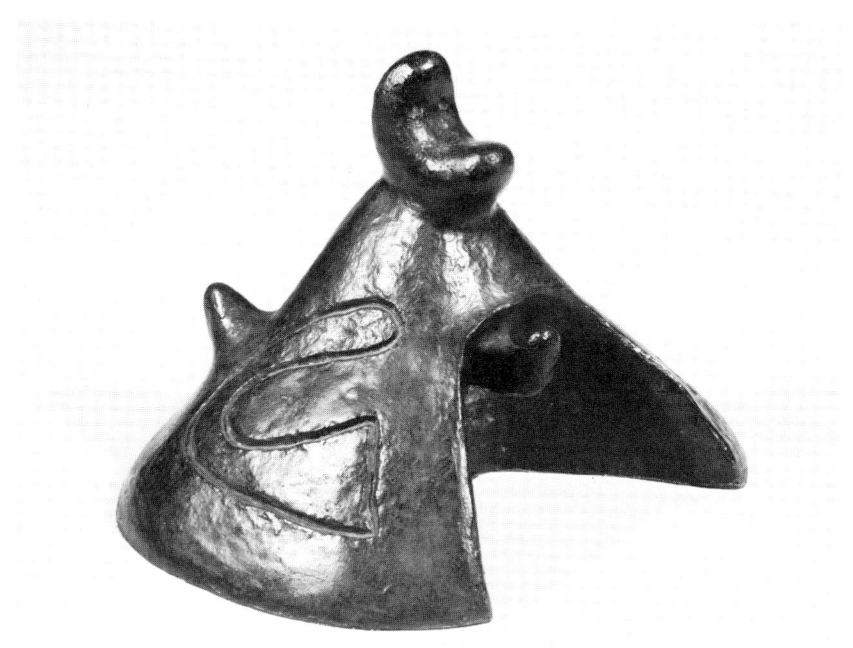

1. FEMME, 1949

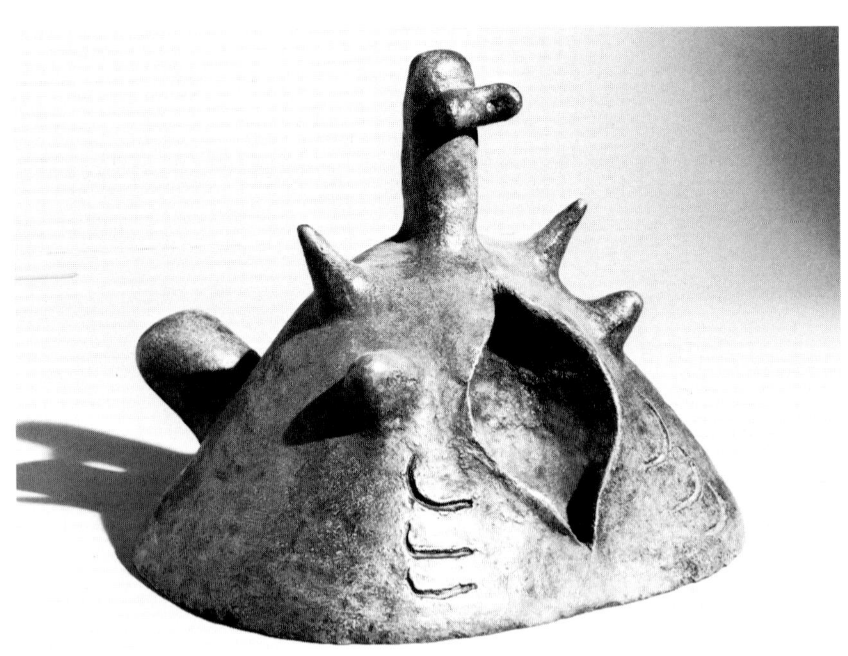

2. FEMME, 1967

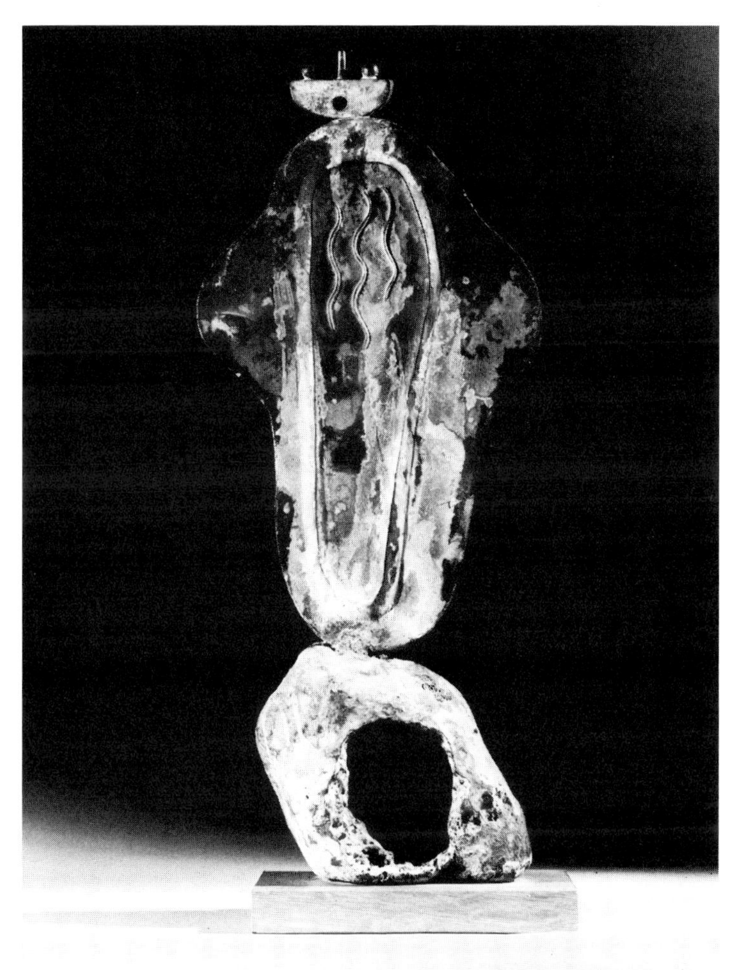

3. FEMME DANS LA NUIT, 1967

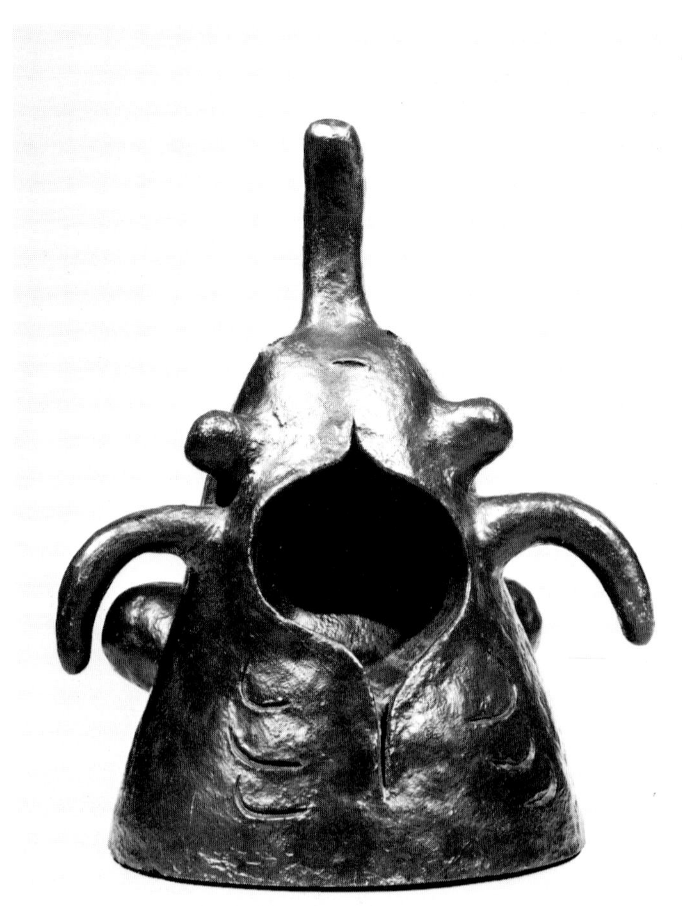

4. FEMME, 1967

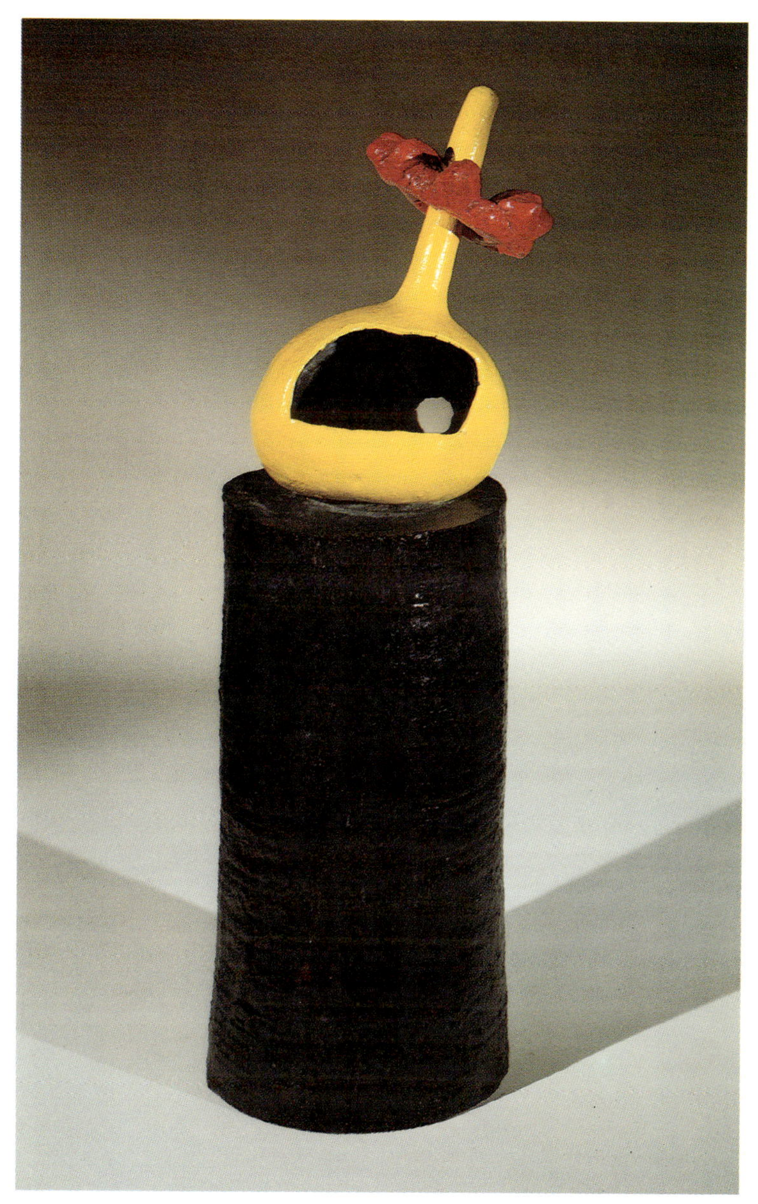

5. SA MAJESTE, 1967-1968

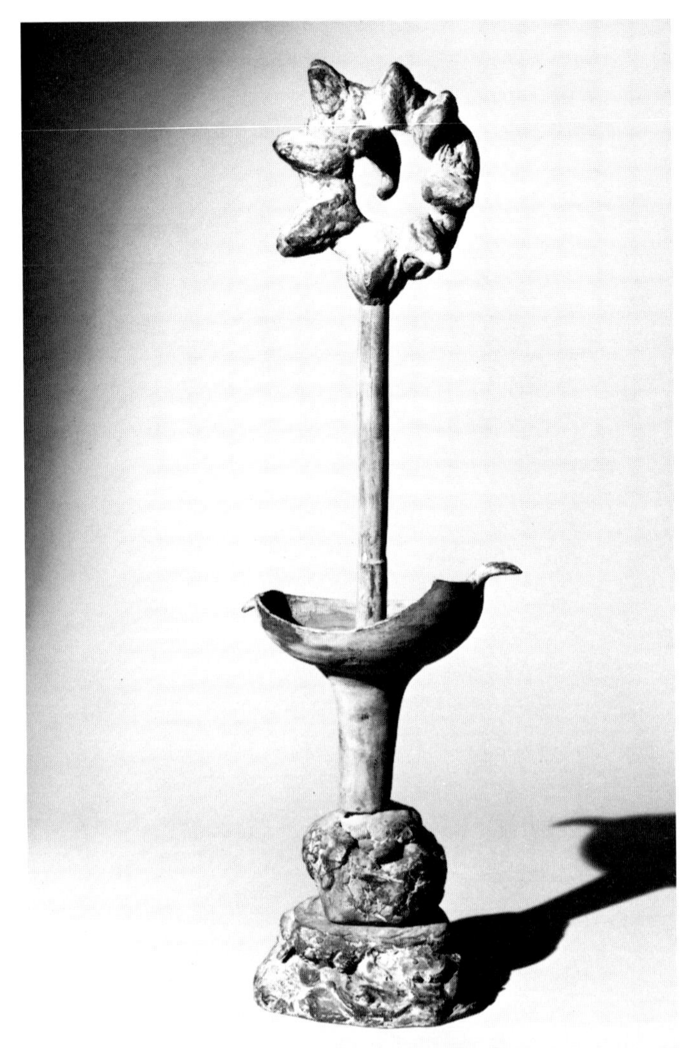

6. FEMME SOLEIL, 1967

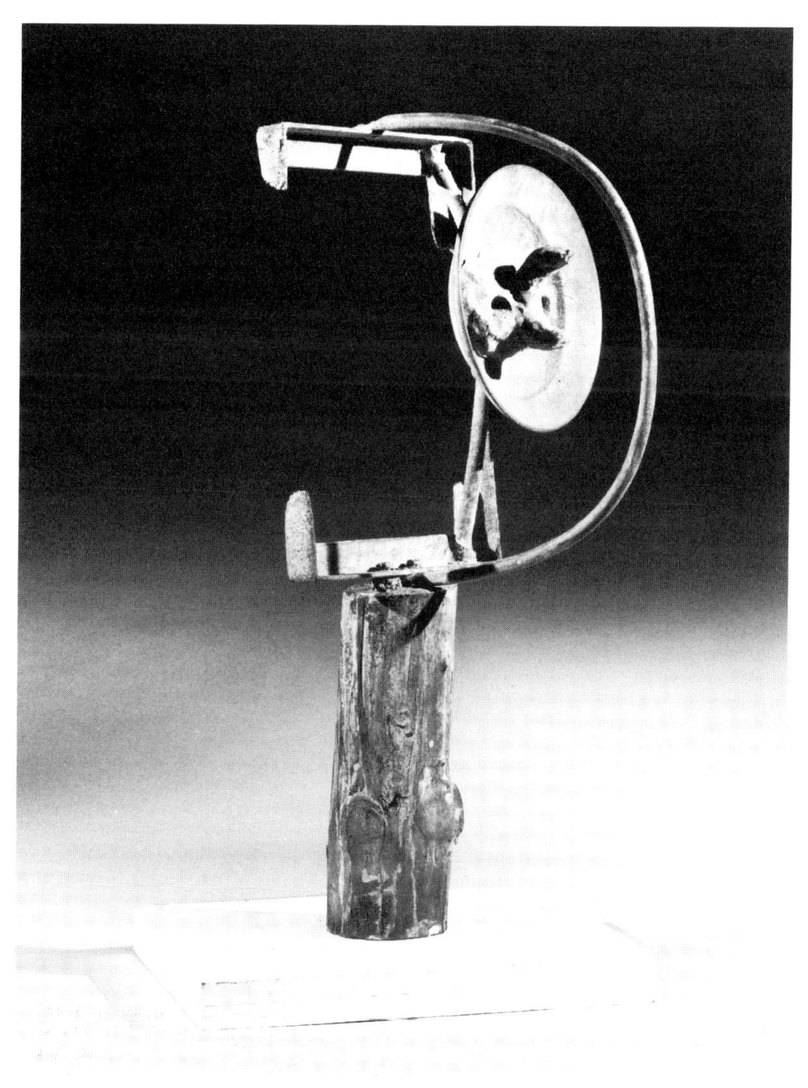

7. TETE DANS LA NUIT, 1968

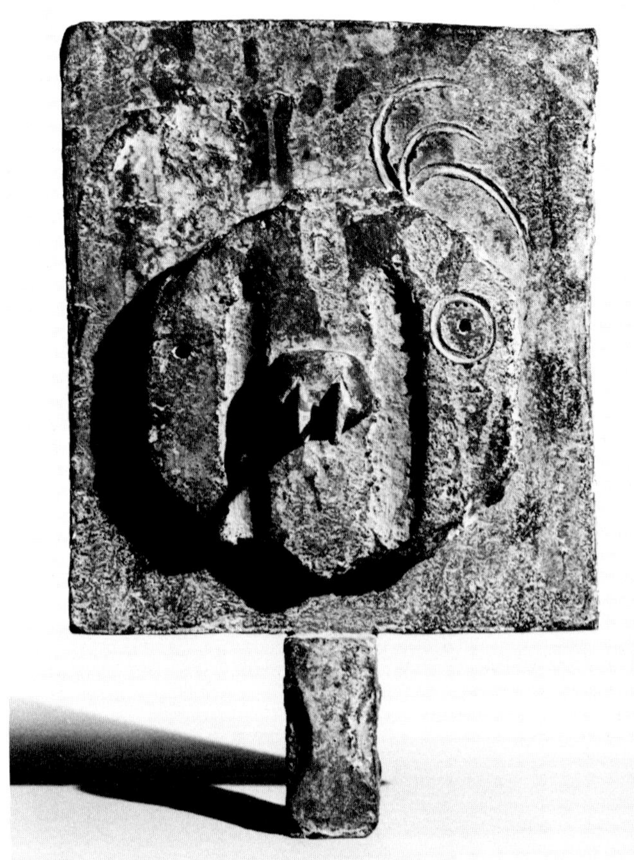

8. TETE, 1968

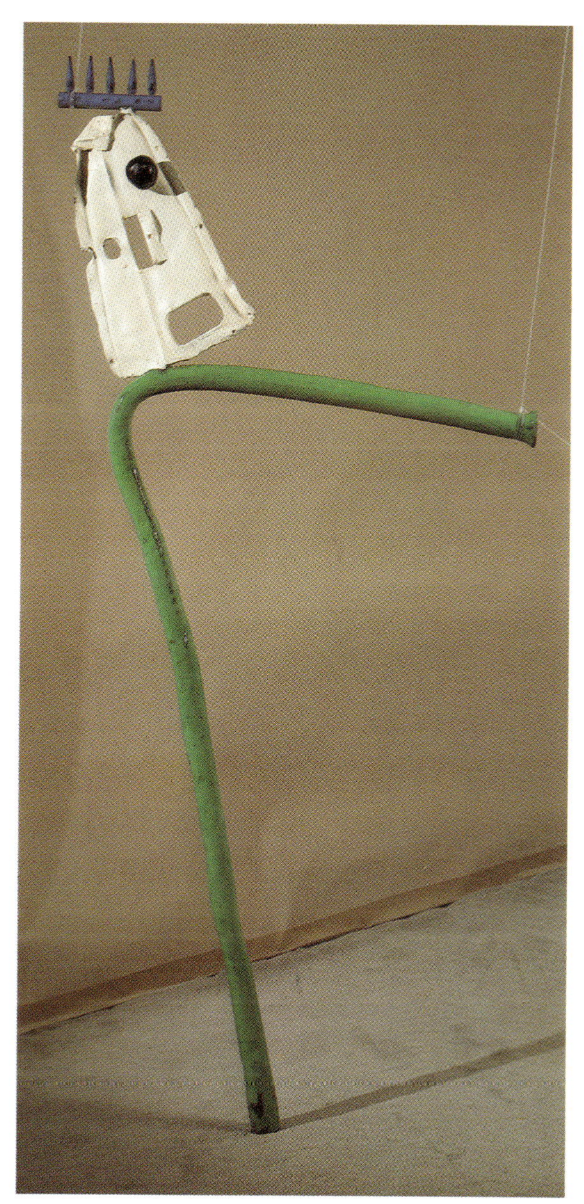

9. PERSONNAGE, 1968

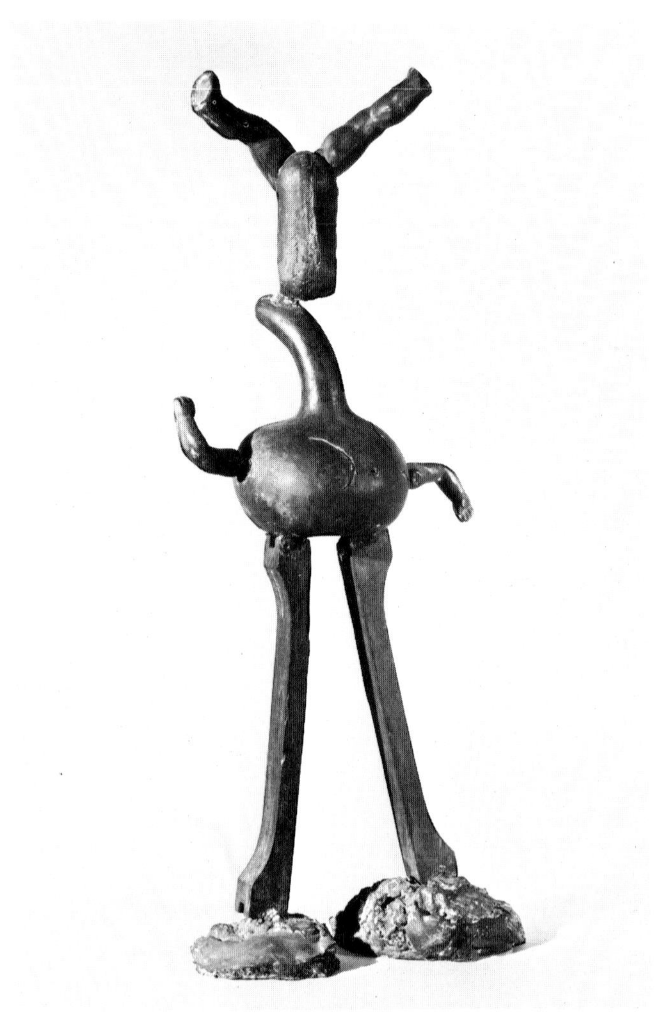

10. L'EQUILIBRISTE, 1969

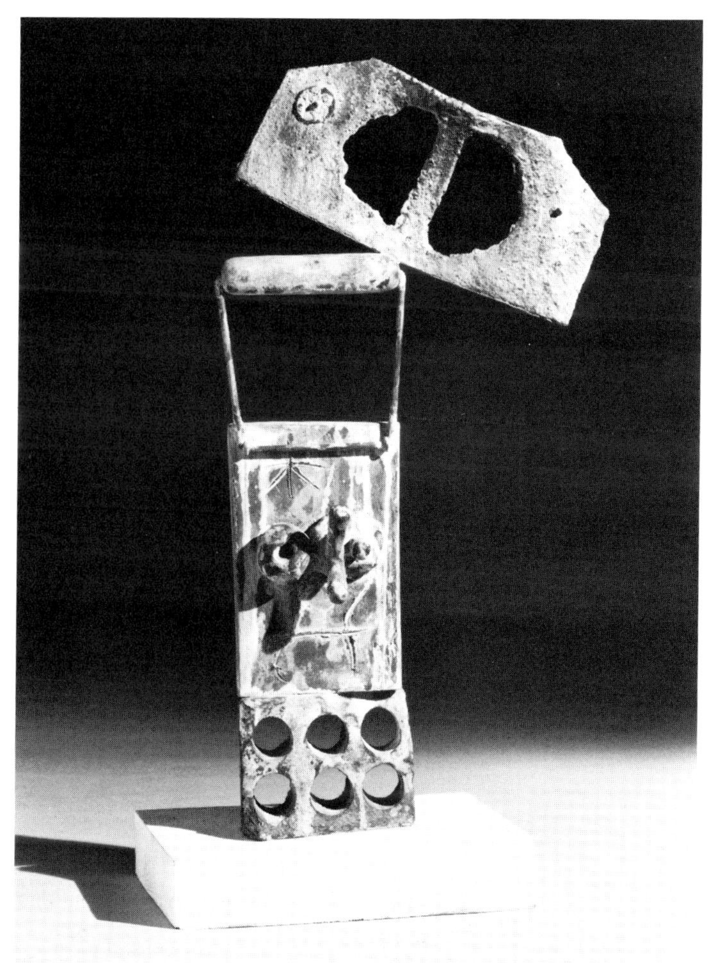

11. TETE, 1969

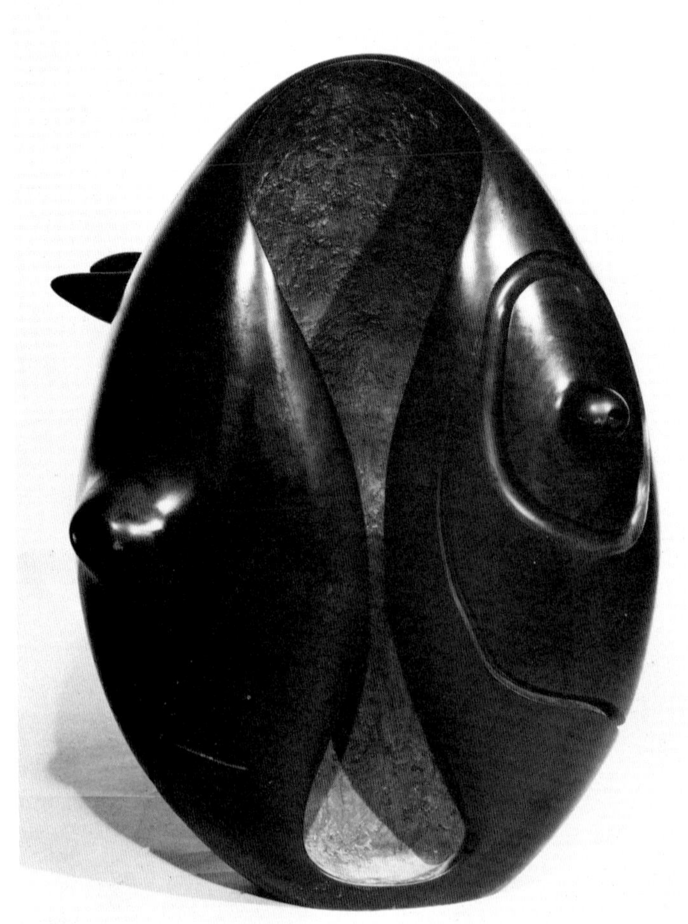

12. CONQUE, 1969

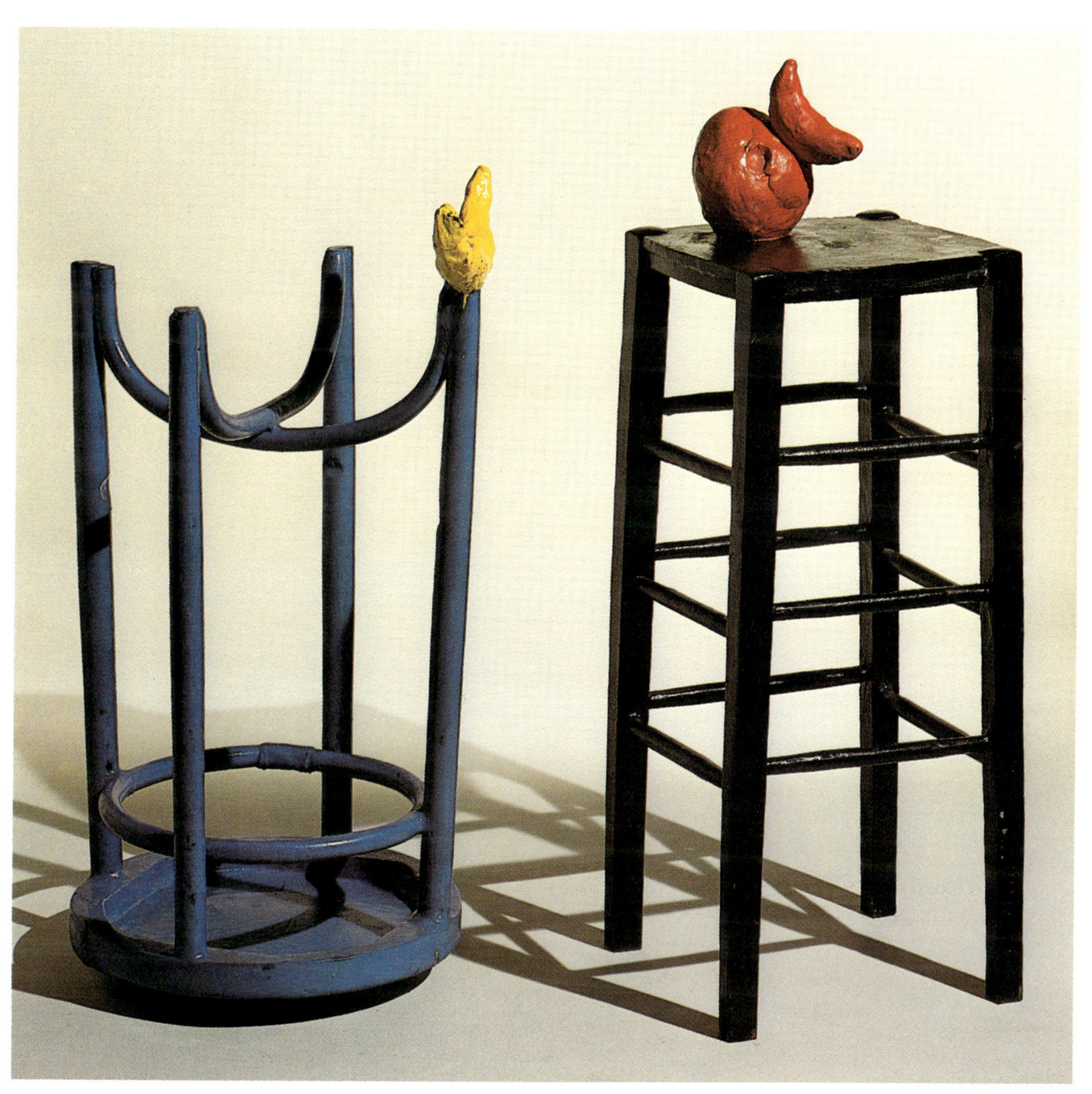

13. HOMME ET FEMME DANS LA NUIT, 1969

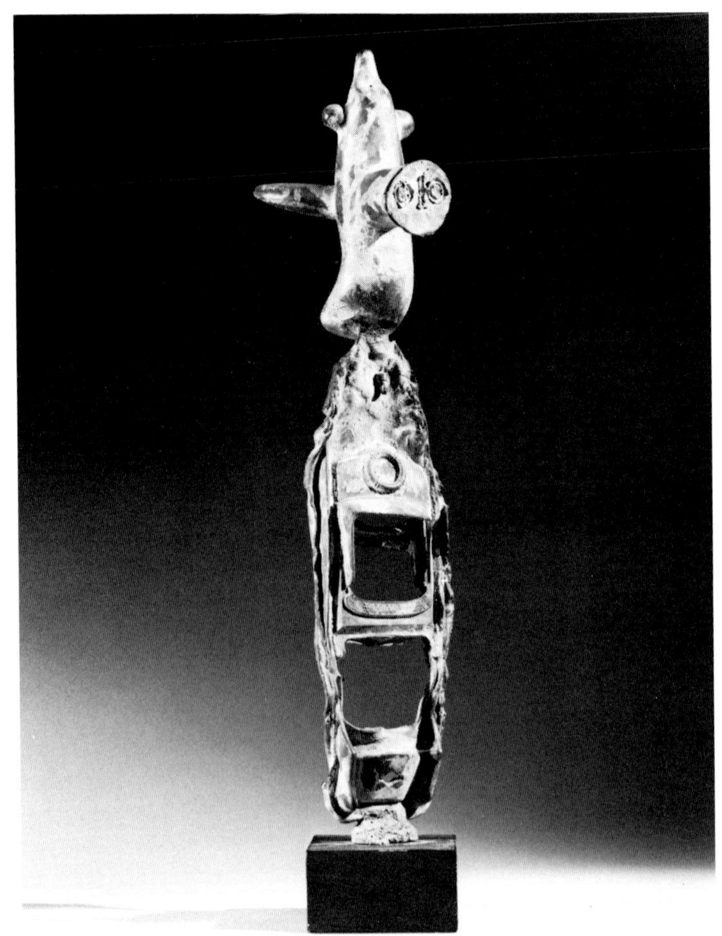

14. PROJET POUR UN MONUMENT, 1969

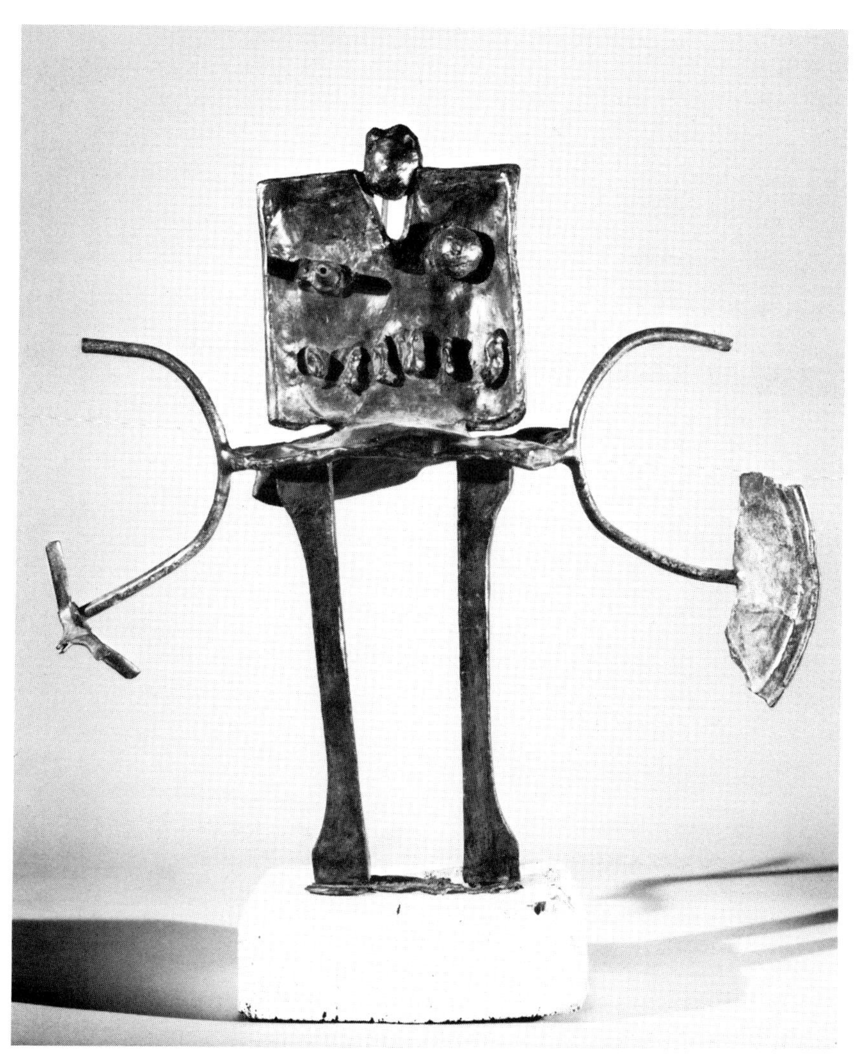

15. FEMME ECHEVELEE, 1969

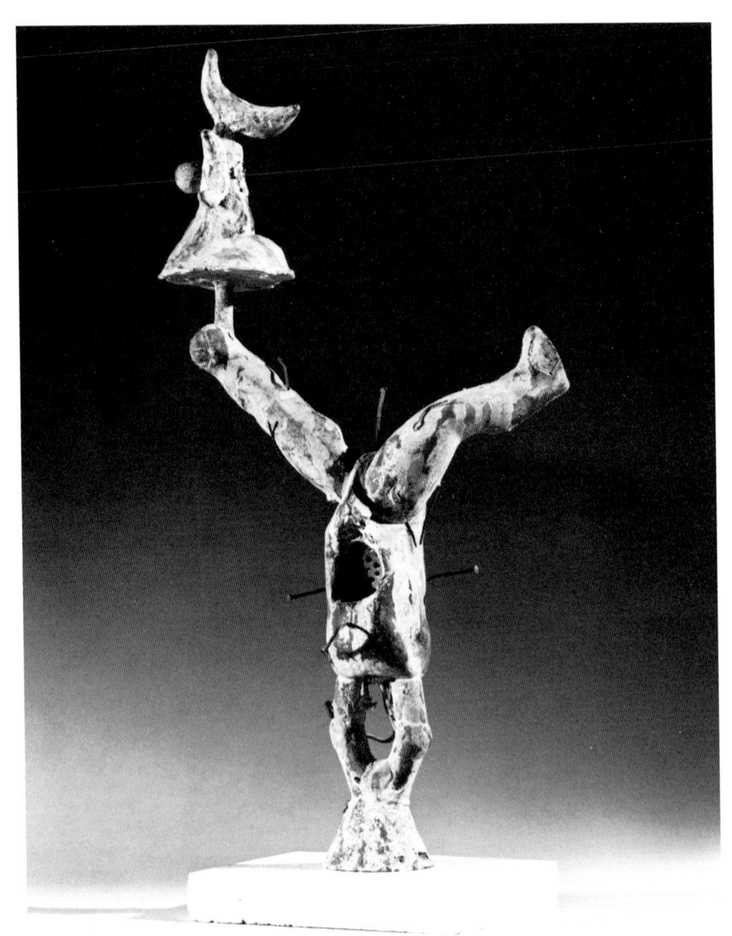

16. L'EQUILIBRISTE, 1970

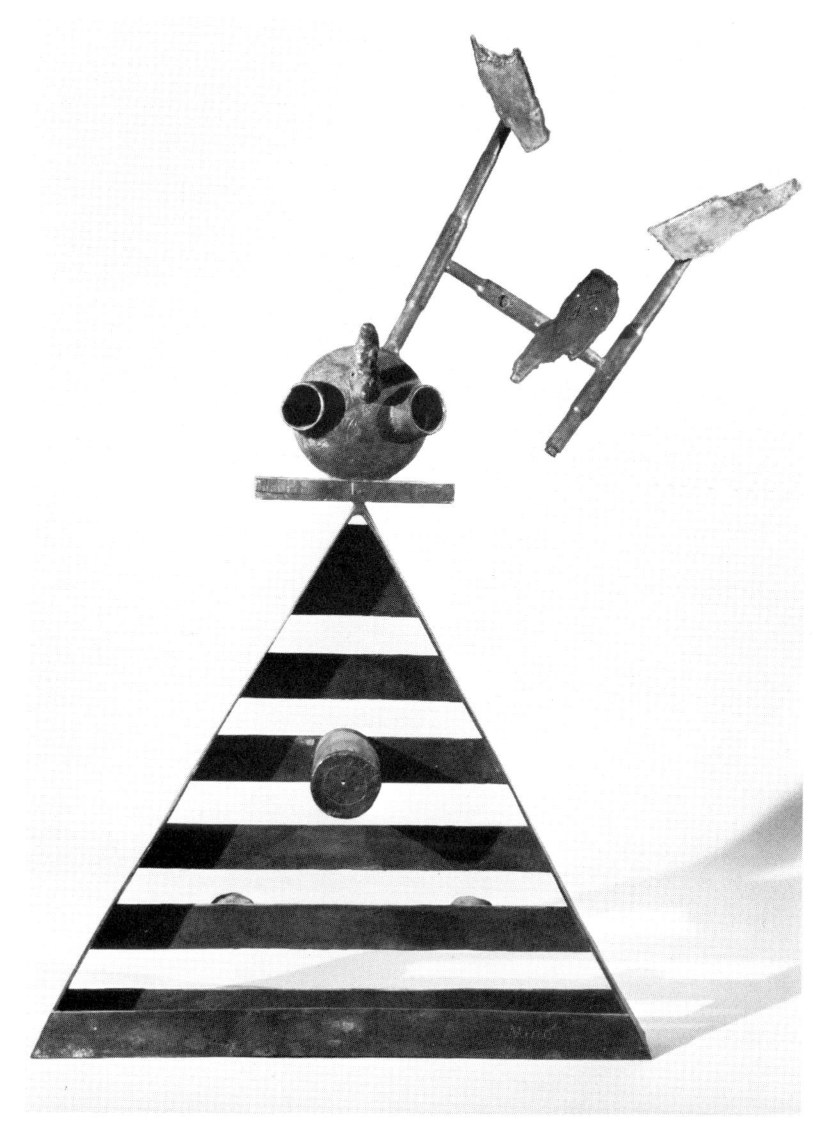

17. PERSONNAGE ET OISEAU, 1970

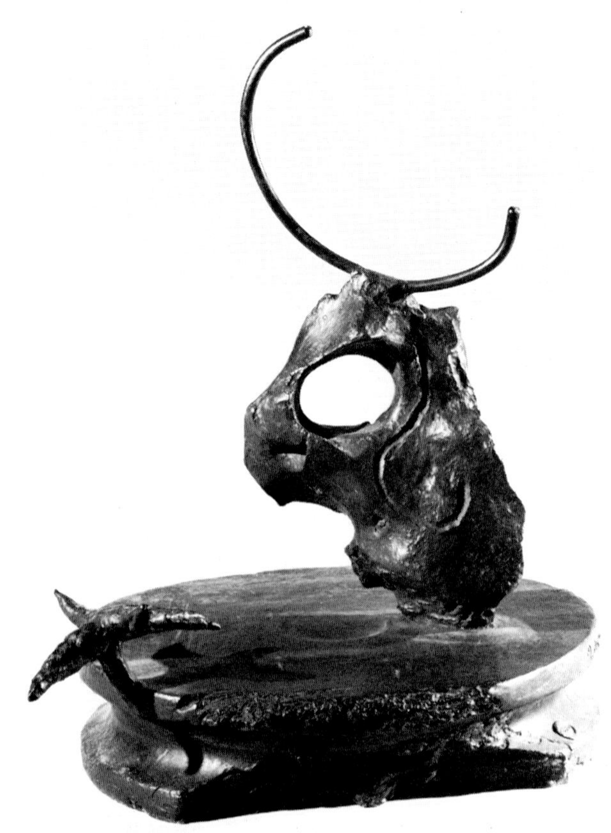

18. TETE ET OISEAU, 1971

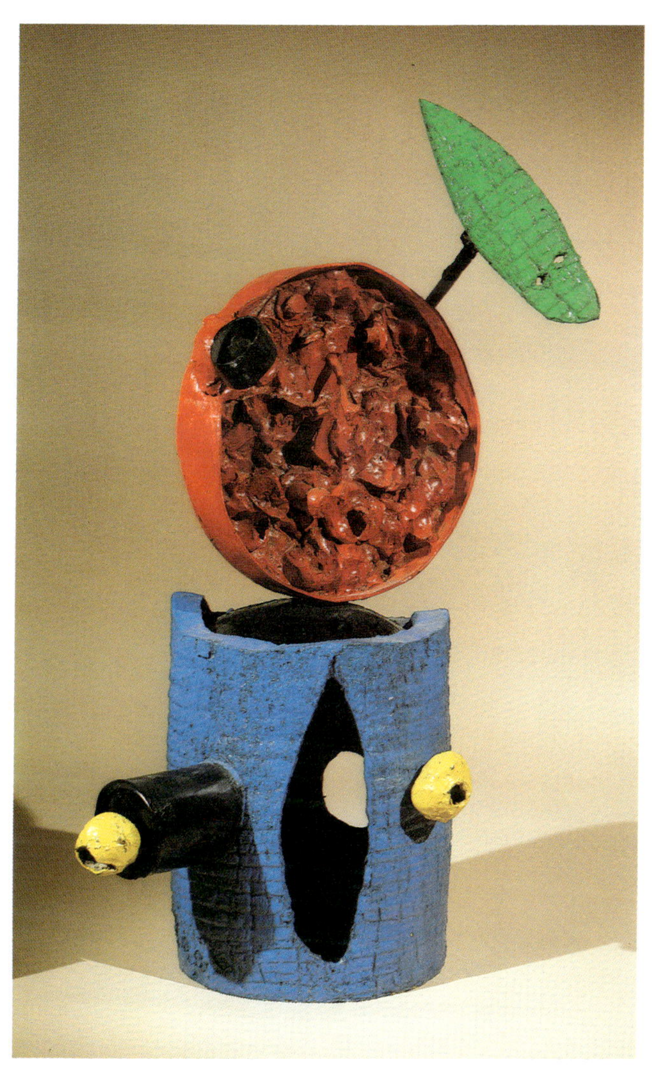

19. FEMME ET OISEAU, 1971

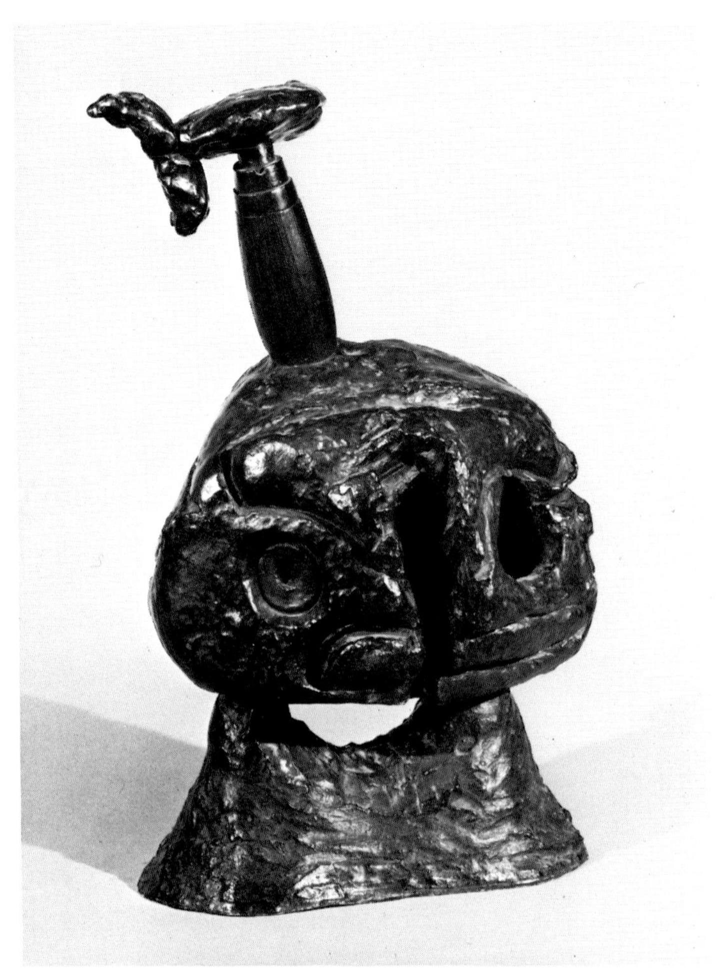

20. FEMME, 1971

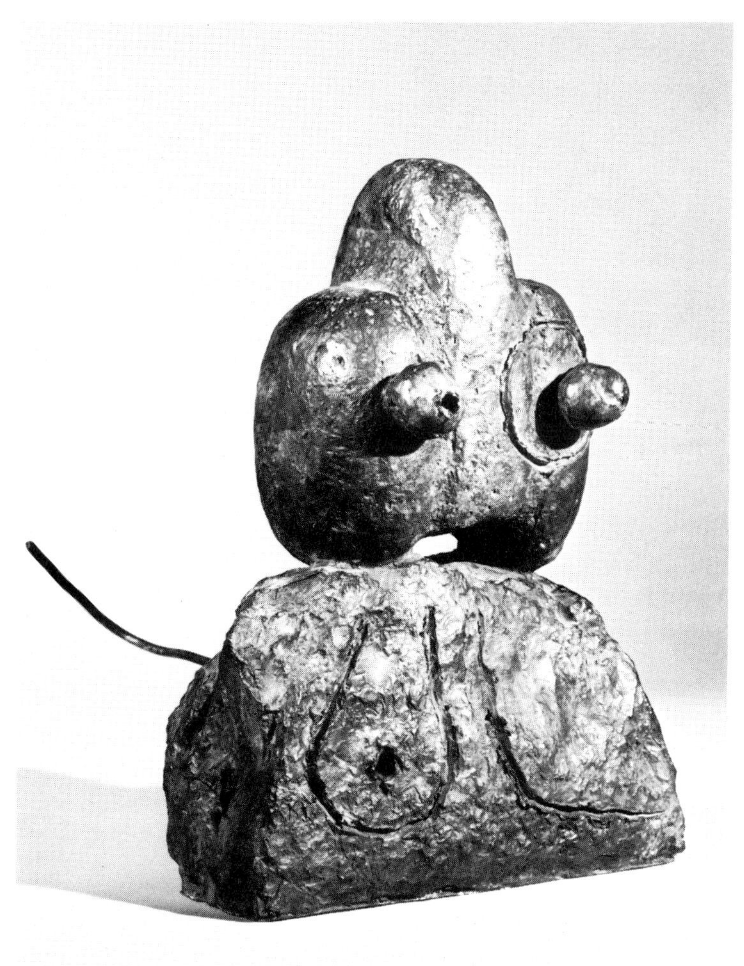

21. FEMME CHIEN, 1972

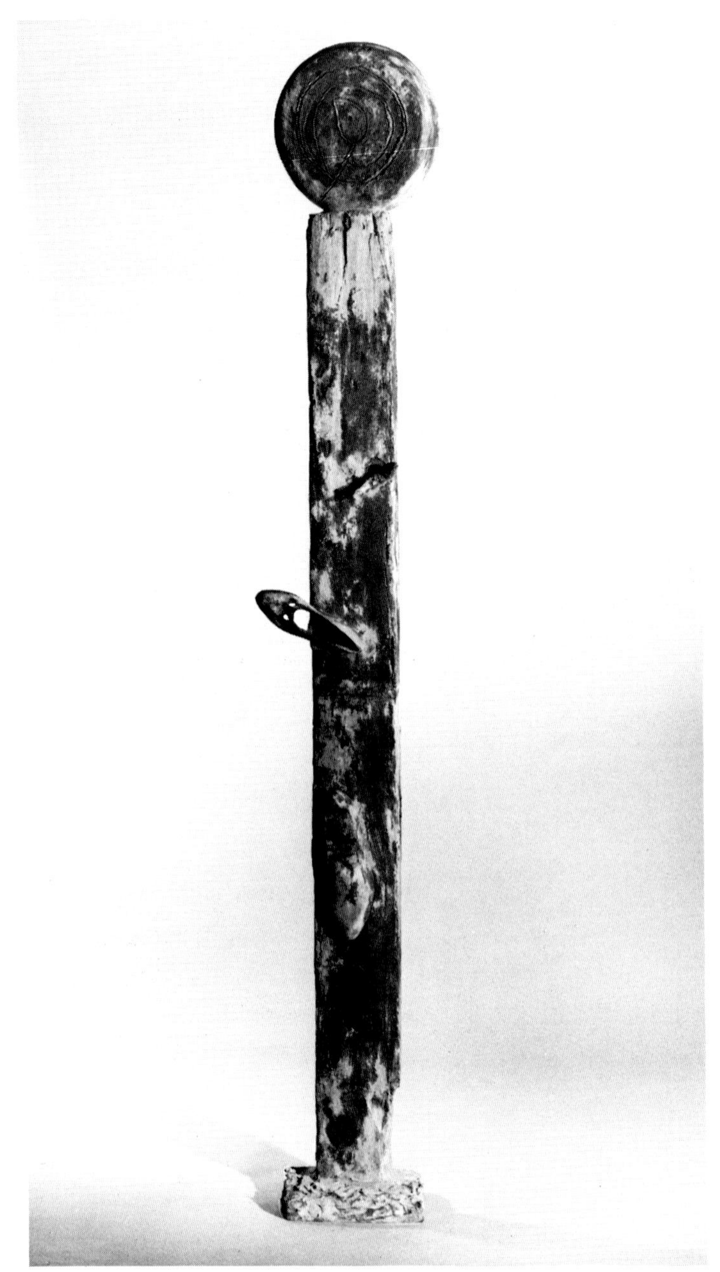

22. TOTEM, 1972

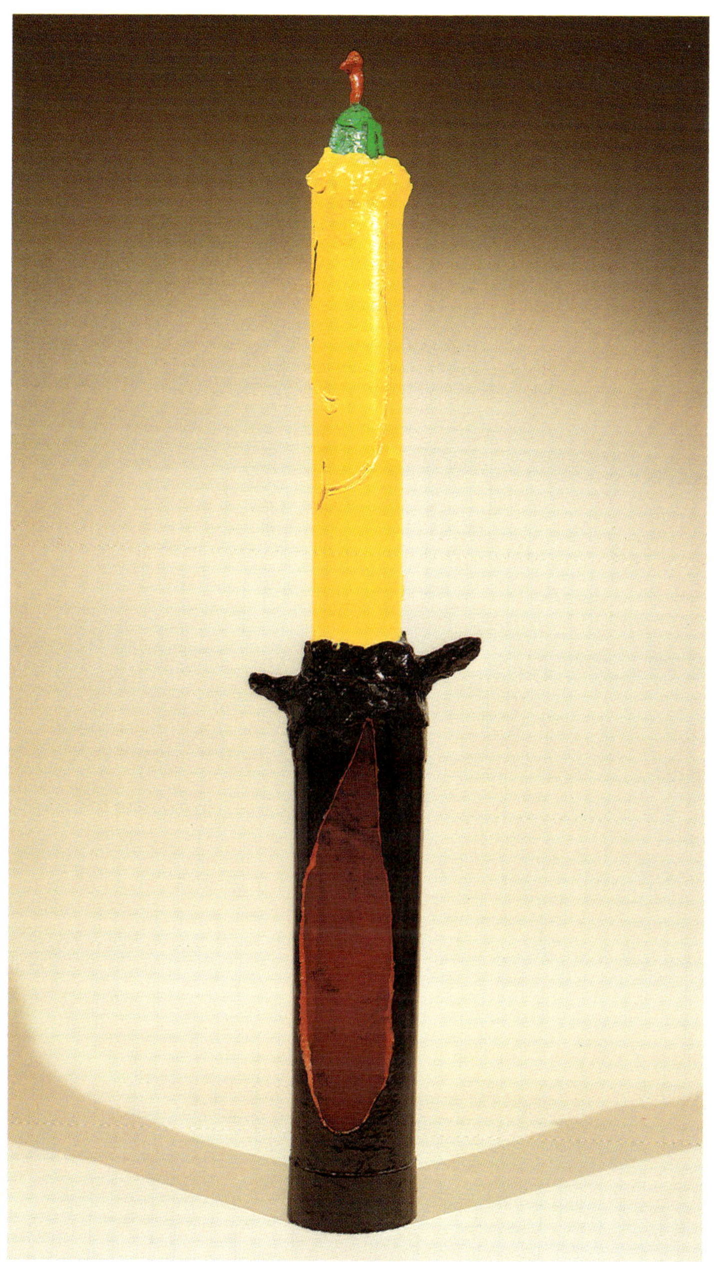

23. PROJET POUR UN MONUMENT, 1973

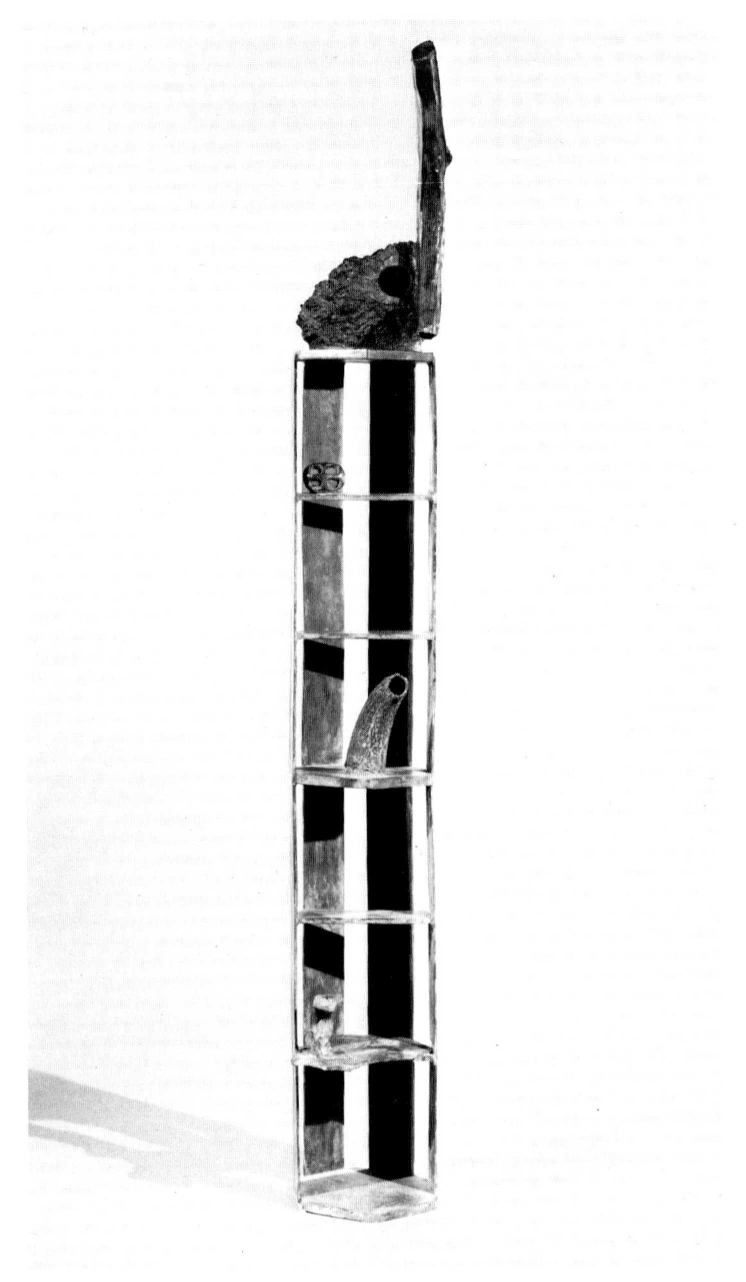

24. PROJET POUR UN MONUMENT, 1973

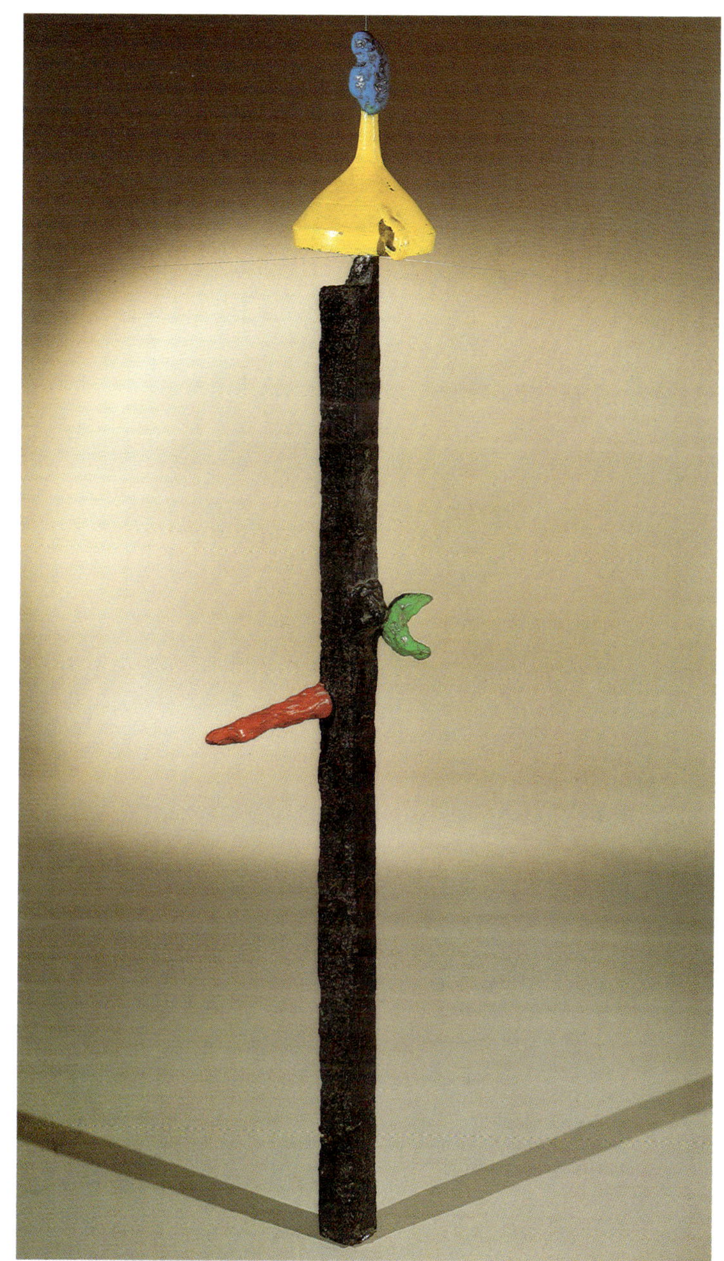

25. FEMME, 1973

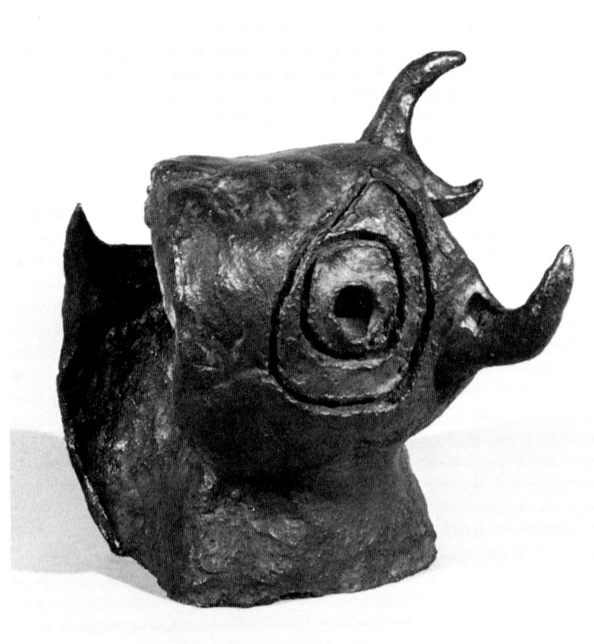

26. TETE, 1975

1. FEMME, 1949.
   bronze, edition: 8.
   21 x 25 x 22 cm./8.3 x 9.8 x 8.7 ins.
   Fonderie V. Gimeno, Barcelone.

2. FEMME, 1967.
   bronze, edition: 6.
   28 x 32 x 26 cm./11 x 12.6 x 10.2 ins.
   Susse-Fondeur, Arcueil.

3. FEMME DANS LA NUIT, 1967.
   bronze, edition: 5.
   64 x 28 x 13 cm./25.2 x 11.5 x 5.1 ins.
   Fonderie Parellada, Barcelone.

4. FEMME, 1967.
   bronze, edition: 6.
   34 x 28 x 22 cm./13.4 x 11 x 8.7 ins.
   Susse-Fondeur, Arcueil.

5. SA MAJESTE, 1967-1968.
   bronze peint/painted bronze, edition: 4.
   120 x 30 x 30 cm./47.2 x 11.8 x 11.8 ins.
   Fonderie T. Clémenti, Meudon.

6. FEMME SOLEIL, 1967.
   bronze, edition: 5.
   86 x 29 x 21.5 cm./33.8 x 11.4 x 8.5 ins.
   Fonderie Parellada, Barcelone.

7. TETE DANS LA NUIT, 1968.
   bronze, edition: 2.
   67.5 x 34.5 x 31 cm./26.6 x 13.6 x 12.2 ins.
   Fonderie Parellada, Barcelone.

8. TETE, 1968.
   bronze, edition: 2.
   39.5 x 26.5 x 12 cm./15.5 x 10.4 x 4.7 ins.
   Fonderie Parellada, Barcelone.

9. PERSONNAGE, 1968.
   bronze peint/painted bronze, edition: 4.
   165 x 65 x 40 cm./64.9 x 25.6 x 15.7 ins.
   Fonderie T. Clémenti, Meudon.

10. L'EQUILIBRISTE, 1969.
    bronze, edition: 2.
    91 x 39 x 18 cm./35.8 x 15.4 x 7 ins.
    Fonderie Parellada, Barcelone.

11. TETE, 1969.
    bronze, edition: 2.
    56 x 30 x 10 cm./22.1 x 11.8 x 3.9 ins.
    Fonderie Parellada, Barcelone.

12. CONQUE, 1969.
    bronze, edition: 6.
    110 x 80 x 50 cm./43.3 x 31.5 x 19.7 ins.
    Susse-Fondeur, Arcueil.

13. HOMME ET FEMME DANS LA NUIT, 1969.
    bronze peint/painted bronze, edition: 4.
    78 x 45 x 45 & 87 x 32 x 32 cm./30.7 x 17.7 x 17.7
    & 34.3 x 12.6 x 12.6 ins.
    Fonderie T. Clémenti, Meudon.

14. PROJET POUR UN MONUMENT, 1969.
    bronze, edition: 2.
    53 x 11.5 x 13 cm./20.9 x 4.5 x 5.1 ins.
    Fonderie Parellada, Barcelone.

15. FEMME ECHEVELEE, 1969.
    bronze, edition: 4.
    70 x 72 x 41 cm./27.6 x 28.3 x 16.1 ins.
    Fonderie T. Clémenti, Meudon.

16. L'EQUILIBRISTE, 1970.
    bronze, edition: 2.
    53 x 30 x 11 cm./20.9 x 11.8 x 4.3 ins.
    Fonderie Parellada, Barcelone.

17. PERSONNAGE ET OISEAU, 1970.
    bronze, edition: 4.
    160 x 122 x 28 cm./63 x 48 x 11 ins.
    Fonderie T. Clémenti, Meudon.

18. TETE ET OISEAU, 1971.
    bronze, edition: 2.
    47.5 x 37 x 33 cm./18.7 x 14.6 x 13 ins.
    Fonderie R. Scuderi, Clamart.

19. FEMME ET OISEAU, 1971.
    bronze peint/painted bronze,
    edition: 2.
    78 x 42 x 42 cm./30.7 x 16.5 x 16.5 ins.
    Fonderie Valsuani et Fils, Bagneux.

20. FEMME, 1971.
    bronze, edition: 2.
    57.5 x 30 x 25 cm./22.6 x 11.8 x 9.8 ins.
    Fonderie R. Scuderi, Clamart.

21. FEMME CHIEN, 1972.
    bronze, edition: 2.
    39 x 38 x 36 cm./15.4 x 15.4 x 14.2 ins.
    Fonderie T. Clémenti, Meudon.

22. TOTEM, 1972.
    bronze, edition: 4.
    210 x 31 x 20 cm./82.7 x 12.2 x 7.8 ins.
    Fonderie T. Clémenti, Meudon.

23. PROJET POUR UN MONUMENT, 1973.
    bronze peint/painted bronze, edition: 2.
    133 x 22 x 28 cm./52.4 x 8.7 x 11 ins.
    Fonderie Valsuani et Fils, Bagneux.

24. PROJET POUR UN MONUMENT, 1973.
    bronze, edition: 2.
    180 x 29.5 x 24 cm./70.9 x 11.6 x 9.4 ins.
    Fonderie T. Clémenti, Meudon.

25. FEMME, 1973.
    bronze peint/painted bronze, edition: 2.
    145 x 29 x 19 cm./57 x 11.4 x 7.5 ins.
    Fonderie Valsuani et Fils, Bagneux.

26. TETE, 1975.
    bronze, edition: 8.
    32 x 36 x 22 cm./12.6 x 14.2 x 8.7 ins.
    Susse-Fondeur, Arcueil.

Biographical Notes

1893	Born in Barcelona on 20 April
1907	Studies at the L'Ecole de Commerce, Barcelona. Attends La Lonja School of Fine Arts.
1910	Takes a job as a clerk with a business establishment in Barcelona.
1912	Enters Gali's Escola d'Art in Barcelona. Learns to draw by sense of touch which was the origin for his vocation as a sculptor. He became acquainted with the painter Enric C. Ricard and the potter Josep Llorens Artigas. He paints his first oil pictures.
1915	Attends drawing sessions at the Sant Lluch circle until 1918. Makes friends with Joan Prats and J.F. Rafols. It is the beginning of his "fauvist" period.
1917	Paints portraits and landscapes around Montroig.
1918	First one-man show at the Dalmau Gallery, Barcelona. Becomes a member of the Agrupacio Courbet, a group of young painters around Artigas. Paints Detallista landscapes.
1919	First visits Paris and makes friends with Picasso
1920	Stays on in Paris and thereafter spends every winter there, summering in Montroig. He rents a studio in rue Blomet next to André Masson's studio. Meets Pierre Reverdy, Max Jacob and Tristan Tzará.
1921	First one-man show in Paris (Gallery La Licorne) organised by Dalmau; preface to the catalogue by Maurice Raynal. Complete failure. Starts work on 'la Ferme' not finished until next year.
1922	Formation of a group around Miró and Masson of Leiris, Limbour, Artaud, Salacrou, Tual. Close friendships, precarious financial existence, serious problems of artistic expression.
1923	Starts work on 'The Tilled Field' which marks a decisive turning point in this work.
1924	Close friendship with Aragon, Breton et Eluard. Starts to take an active part in the Surrealist exhibitions.
1925	Starts an important series of paintings 'Oneiric' until 1927.
1926	Collaborates with Max Ernst on the sets for 'Romeo and Juliet' for Diaghilev's Ballet Russes. At Montroig during the summers of 1926 and 1927 paints 'Imaginary landscapes'.
1927	Moves studio to the Rue Tourlaque in Montmartre, where he is a neighbour of Max Ernst, Eluard, Arp and Magritte. Works on the themes for 'Cheval de Cirque' and 'Fonds Blancs'.
1928	Visits Holland. Back in Paris, paints Dutch interiors from postcards of old Dutch masters. Large exhibition at the Bernheim Gallery. First papiers collés and collages.
1929	Marries Pilar Juncosa at Palma. Lives in Paris at 3 rue Francois Mouthon.
1930	Makes first lithographs; illustrations for Tristan Tzará's 'L'Arbre des

voyageurs'. During the summer makes the first 'constructions'
assemblages of broken boxes and a variety of objects. First exhibition in
USA at Valentine Gallery, New York.

1931   Birth of his daughter Dolores.
Exhibition of sculpture-objects at Galerie Pierre, Paris.

1932   Designs sets, costumes, curtain and "toys" for the ballet 'Jeux d'enfant',
choreographed by Massine for the Ballets de Monte Carlo. In the summer
worked on a series of small paintings on wood.
First exhibition in November at the Pierre Matisse Gallery, New York.
Exhibits with the Surrealists at the Salon des Surindépendants.

1933   First etchings: illustrations for 'Enfaces' by Georges Hugnet.
Drawing-collages. Big paintings executed from collages exhibited at the
Bernheim Gallery in October.

1934   Miró's "savage" period begins.

1936   Paints small paintings in tempera and oil on copper. In the Autumn Miró
leaves Spain with his family and lives in Paris.

1937   Lives at a hotel in the Rue Jules Chaplain. Later finds apartment in the
Boulevard Blanqui. Attends drawing classes from the nude model at the
Grande Chaumière. *Still Life with an Old Shoe, Self-Portrait,* poster for the
Spanish Loyalists. *The Reaper* painted for the Spanish Pavilion at the Paris
World Fair, 1938.

1938   Writes "Je rêve d'un grand atelier." Many paintings in a somewhat calmer,
more austere manner. Engravings and drypoints done in Marcoussis'
studio. Summer at Varengeville in Normandy.

1939   Music now inspires the painter as formerly poetry had done. Spends the
summer at Varengeville. *Flight of a Bird over the Plain* series and paintings
on burlap.

1940   Begins the series of *Constellations* at Varengeville during the first months
of the war. On May 20th, in the face of the advancing German army, returns
to Paris and then moves on to Spain. Settles temporarily at Palma.

1941   Finishes the *Constellations* in Palma and Montroig. The Museum of
Modern Art in New York holds a big retrospective of Miró's work. First
monograph on Miró written by James Johnson Sweeney.

1942   Back in Barcelona, living in the Pasaje del Credito. Attempts to achieve a
more austere style. Works on paper to 1944.

1944   Miró's mother dies. "Barcelona" series of lithographs. First ceramics with
the assistance of Artigas. Small paintings in his new manner.

1945   Exhibition of *Constellations* and some ceramics at the Pierre Matisse
Gallery, New York. Series of large paintings on white and black grounds.

1946   Many paintings, including the series called *Woman and Bird in the Night*.

1947   First trip to the United States. Mural painting for the Terrace Hilton Hotel
in Cincinnati. In New York at Hayter's Studio 17 makes a number of
etchings, including illustrations for *L'Antitête* by Tristan Tzará. Exhibition

at the Pierre Matisse Gallery. Represented in the Surrealist exhibition, Galerie Maeght.

1948   Returns to Paris. Exhibition at the Galerie Maeght. Begins a series of prints at Lacourrière's and makes lithographs at Mourlot's, notably *Album 13* and illustrations for *Parlez seul* by Tristan Tzará.

1949   Exhibition in Barcelona of works owned by local collectors. Retrospective at the Kunsthalle, Bern. During this year and the next, produces a series of works called "slow" and "spontaneous."

1950   Moves from the Pasaje del Credito to the Calle Fulgarolas. Makes his first wood-cuts for *Miró* by Cabral de Melo. Exhibition of paintings and sculptures at the Galerie Maeght. Mural painting for Harvard University.

1952   This year and the next executes many pictures in a freer, more brutal style, the most important of which is the big 1953 canvas in the Guggenheim Museum. Exhibition at the Kunsthalle, Basel.

1953   Exhibitions at the Galerie Maeght, the Pierre Matisse Gallery, and at the Kunsthalle, Bern.

1954   Travelling exhibition, German museums. Participates in the Venice Biennale; awarded Grand Prix International for graphic work. The many paintings of this period terminate a stage in his development, and apart from a few small works on cardboard done in 1955, Miró stops painting until 1959.

1955   Second stage of work in ceramics with Artigas, begun in 1954 and finished in 1956.

1956   Exhibitions of ceramics at the Galerie Maeght and the Pierre Matisse Gallery. Big retrospective in Brussels, Amsterdam, and Basel. Moves family and studio from Barcelona to Palma, where he occupies a big modern studio designed by J.L. Sert.

1957   Works on two ceramic walls for the UNESCO building in Paris (completed in 1958). Graphic work exhibited in German museums.

1958   Participates in the exhibition "Fifty Years of Modern Art" at the Brussels World Fair. Prints executed at the Crommelynck studio for René Crevel's *La Bague d'aurore*, and René Char's *Nous avons*. Illustrates Paul Eluard's *A toute épreuve* with 80 woodcuts. Print entitled *The Giants* introduces a new style. UNESCO walls win the Guggenheim International Award.

1959   Second trip to the United States, in connection with retrospective shows at the Museum of Modern Art, New York and the Los Angeles Museum. Resumes painting.

1960   "New Paintings." With Artigas executes a ceramic mural for Harvard University, exhibited first in Barcelona, Paris, and New York. Engravings and lithographs in the Maeght studio, many for *Album 19*, with a preface by Raymond Queneau.

1961   Mural paintings, *Blue I, II,* and *III*. Exhibition of the "New Paintings" at Galerie Maeght. Exhibition at Pierre Matisse Gallery. Third visit to the

United States. Exhibition of graphic work, Geneva.

1962   Retrospective at the National Museum of Modern Art in Paris. Exhibition of graphic work at the Museum of Modern Art, Tokyo. Continues on the series, started in 1959, of paintings on torn and perforated cardboard.

1964   Inauguration of the Foundation Maeght at Saint-Paul and the garden and labyrinth is decorated with Miró's sculptures and ceramics. One room is devoted to his painting. Retrospective exhibitions at the Tate Gallery and at the Kunsthaus, Zurich. Ceramique mural for the L'Ecole superieure de Commerce of Saint-Gall. Participates in Documenta III at Kassel.

1966   Makes first monumental sculptures in bronze *'L'Oiseau Solaire'* and *'L'Oiseau Lunaire'*. One-man exhibition of paintings 1956-66 at the Marlborough Gallery, London. Grand retrospective at the National Museum of Modern Art, Tokyo touring to the Museum of Modern Art, Kyoto. Miró visits Japan on this occasion.
Exhibition of his complete graphic work at the Philadelphia Museum.
Executes a large ceramic mural for the Guggenheim Museum in New York.

1967   Carnegie prize for painting.
Commenced a series of sculptures in bronze for which he employs a number of 'objets trouvés'.
Exhibition of *'L'Oiseau solaire, L'Oiseau Lunaire, etincelles'* at Galerie Maeght, Paris touring to the Pierre Matisse Gallery, New York.

1968   Large retrospective exhibition on his 75th birthday at Foundation Maeght and touring to the Old Hospital at Santa Cruez, Barcelona.

1969   Retrospective exhibition at the Haus der Kunst, Munich.
Exhibition 'Miro Otro' organised by the young architects of Barcelona.

1970   Executes a ceramic mural for Barcelona airport and painted and ceramic murals for the International Exhibition Centre in Osaka, Japan.
Exhibition of sculptures 1967-70 at the Pierre Matisse Gallery, New York and Galerie Maeght, Paris.
Participates in the exhibition 'Metamorphose de l'object' organised by the Palais des Beaux-Arts, Brussels (and touring around Europe).
Exhibition of sculpture at Galleria Arte Borgogna, Milan.

1971   Exhibition of paintings, sculptures and ceramics at the Casino, Knokke-Le-Zoute.
In homage to his friend Joan Prats, an exhibition of lithographs at Sala Gaspar, Barcelona.
Touring exhibition of sculptures organised by the Walker Art Centre, Minneapolis, then the Museum of Art, Cleveland and the Art Institute of Chicago.

1972   Exhibition 'Miro Bronzes' Hayward Gallery, London
Exhibition 'Sobreteixims i escultures' at Sala Gaspar, Barcelona
Exhibition 'Das plastische Werk' Kunsthaus, Zurich
Retrospective Exhibition, Liljevalchs Konstall, Stockholm
Exhibition 'Magnetic Fields' Guggenheim Museum, New York (then touring around USA).

1973	Exhibition 'Sobreteixims' Galerie Maeght, Paris.
	Large exhibition of sculptures and ceramics at Foundation Maeght.
1974	Retrospective exhibition at Grand Palais, Paris.
	Exhibition at Louisiana Museum of Modern Art, Copenhagen.
	Exhibition of the complete graphic work at the Museum of Modern Art, Hotel de la Ville, Paris.
1975	Exhibition of the complete graphic work at Foundation Gulbenkian, Lisbonne.
	Exhibition of sculptures, Galerie Schmela, Düsseldorf.
	Opening of the Miró Foundation in Barcelona. Designed by the architect Joseph Sert this foundation was to be for Miró, more than a museum, a living centre of contemporary art (exhibitions, cinema, music, architecture and Catalan culture.
	First exhibition of recent work from his foundry.
1976	Execution of a ceramic wall for IBM in Barcelona. Preparation of an enormous mosaic for the Museum in Ludwigshafen.
1977	Exhibition at Museum of Ceret, Pyrenees-Orientales.
	Completed a mosaic of 15.80 metres wide by 8 metres high 'Personnages et oiseau' in marble and glass for Wichita State University's McKnight Art Center, USA and also a giant tapestry for the National Gallery, Washington.
1978	Executed a sculpture in synthetic resin for the walk of 'La Defense' in Paris.
	Retrospective exhibition to commemorate his 85th birthday at the Spanish Museum of Contemporary Art in Madrid and an exhibition of his graphic work at Salas de la Dirección General Del Patrimonio Aristico de Madrid.
	Exhibition at Galerie Theo, Madrid.
	Exhibition of drawing, gouaches and large sculpture and intimate ceramics 'Homage to Josep Llorens Artigas' Galerie Maeght, Barcelona.
	Designed sets and costumes for the spectacle at the Theatre de la Claca 'Mori et Merma' touring to the Theatre Tinell in Barcelona and the Theatre in the Georges Pompidou Centre in Paris on the occasion of the opening of a large exhibition of drawings.
	Exhibition of recent paintings, Galerie Maeght, Paris.
	Retrospective exhibition of sculpture at the Museum d'art moderne, Hotel de la Ville, Paris.
	Retrospective exhibition, Palma de Majorca.
	Exhibition of small works, Pierre Matisse Gallery, New York.
1979	During this year an exhibition of sculptures toured Japan.
	Exhibitions at Florence and Siena.
	Exhibition of painting, sculpture and drawings at Foundation Maeght, Saint Paul.
	Sculpture exhibition, Museum Saint-Georges, Liege.
1980	Sculpture exhibition, Amos Anderson Museum, Helsinki.
	Exhibition Isetan Museum, Tokyo.
	Retrospective exhibition Museum of Modern Art, Tokyo.

1981   An exhibition of paintings, sculptures, collages, ceramics and tapestries
        throughout the museums and galleries of all of Milan from October – November.
        Exhibition of sculptures at Waddington Galleries, London.

Select Bibliography

Joan Miró Arts Council, Tate Gallery, 1964
Miró Sculptures Walker Art Center, Minneapolis, 1971
Miró Bronzes Arts Council, Hayward Gallery, 1972
Joan Miró: Das plastische Werk, Kunsthaus Zurich, 1972
Joan Miró: Peintures, Sculptures, Dessins, Céramiques 1956-1979 Fondation Maeght, 1979
Joan Miró: Scultura 1931-1972 Palazzo Pretorio, Prato, 1979
Joan Miró: Painted Sculpture and Ceramics, Pierre Matisse Gallery, New York, 1980.
Miró Sculptures, Alain Jouffroy and Joan Teixidor, Maeght éditeur, 1980: includes a
complete catalogue of Miró's sculpture, other than work in ceramics, up to 1979.